Fear Free

Another Destiny Image Book by
Bill Dennington

Breaking the Strongholds of Iniquity: A New Testament Guide to Cleansing Your Generational Bloodline

Fear Free

KEYS TO DEFEATING THE STRONGHOLD OF FEAR IN YOUR LIFE

BILL DENNINGTON

DESTINY IMAGE® PUBLISHERS, INC.
PO Box 310, Shippensburg, PA 17257-0310
"Promoting Inspired Lives"

This book and all other Destiny Image and Destiny Image Fiction books are available at Christian bookstores and distributors worldwide.

Cover design by: Eileen Rockwell

For more information on foreign distributors, call 717-532-3040.

Or reach us on the Internet: www.destinyimage.com

ISBN 13 TP: 978-0-7684-5685-1

ISBN 13 eBook: 978-0-7684-5686-8

For Worldwide Distribution.

1 2 3 4 5 6 / 23 22 21 20

Contents

Introduction 9

Session 1 Where Does Fear Come From? 13

Session 2 Different Types of Fear. 27

Session 3 Step One to Freedom: Securing a
           New Identity 49

Session 4 Step Two to Freedom: Renewing
           the Mind 71

Session 5 Step Three to Freedom: Act on the
           Word, Even When Facing Fear. . 91

About the Author 99

Introduction

The world we live in today is a world virtually dominated by fear. Frequent events reported in the news of our day are terror attacks and major natural disasters. Life-threatening diseases that can very quickly reach pandemic levels on a worldwide scale are becoming common occurrences, right along with major economic disruptions that stress governments from local to national levels.

How do you as a born-again believer live a victorious life of faith in the middle of these fear-dominated times? Does God have a way for us to live free from the influence of the world and its anxiety and fear-based stress? Is there peace for your mind in the middle of raging storms?

In this course you will learn what the Word of God has to say about these and related questions you may have. You will learn what the origin of fear is and how to recognize the tale-tell signs of fear. You will see that fear is *not* from God—it is a weapon that our enemy uses to steal the Word out of our heart and open legal pathways into our lives to land the curse—from which we are redeemed.

I encourage you to take notes and go through this course several times to get the most out of it. You need to apply the steps and take advantage of all the spiritual tools and strategies that are made very clear in each of the four sessions. This is not a one shot and done project—it is a mind-re-newing, powerful tool of discipline that I promise you will produce permanent freedom from fear in your life!

So, let's get started and begin your journey to *Freedom From Fear!*

Session 1

Where Does Fear Come From?

Fear has been around for such a long time that many people think it is natural to the human race; that God created fear to serve as a means of alerting humankind to danger. It is so much a part of the human experience that our everyday talk uses expressions of many different types of fear, ranging from expressing concern to being completely terrified.

No doubt, fear is a powerful force and can actually do harm to our minds, emotions, and bodies. Living in constant fear is not a healthy lifestyle and can break down our body's immune system and even cause people to lose and even change the color of their hair. Fear can disrupt the digestive tract and cause all manner of physical issues.

The one common-across-the-board symptom of fear in people's lives is a lack of peace. It is a disruptive and destructive force that causes misery and can lead to an untimely death. So, where does fear come from and where did it originate?

To understand where fear finds its origins, we need to turn to the Bible and the book of Isaiah, chapter 54, verses 14-15:

> *In righteousness **you shall be established; you shall be far from oppression, for you shall not fear; and from terror, for it shall not come near you. Indeed they shall surely assemble, but***

not because of Me. *Whoever assembles against you shall fall for your sake.*

Notice the bolded part of this Scripture passage. Oppression, fear, and terror will gather together against us, but not because the Lord is doing it. Also, the intended purpose of our being made righteous through union with Jesus is to position us in that righteousness to be free from the fear and the oppression it causes and far from terror, too! More on this a little later in the course.

The phrase, *"fear not"* is used 170 times in the King James Version of the Bible. It is a command, not a suggestion; and most of the time it is being spoken by angels sent from God, or by God Himself. God is not the source of fear; if He were, it would not make sense for Him to command us not to be afraid.

One important understanding I want to open up to you at this point has to do with the King James Bible version and earlier translations of the Bible's use of the word "fear" in relation to our heart attitude and response to the Lord. The use of the word "fear" in this way is better understood by replacing it with the word "honor." Having a reverential honor of the Lord is a good thing. Being afraid of the Lord is not. We will learn why later.

So who is attempting to impose fear upon us? Take a look at Hebrews 2:14-15 to get some insight into this question:

> *Inasmuch then as the children have partaken of flesh and blood, He Himself likewise shared in the same, that through death He might destroy **him who had the power of death, that is, the devil,***

***and release those who through fear of
death were all their lifetime subject
to bondage.***

Fear is from the devil. It is the result of
perverting faith for evil and wicked pur-
poses resulting in iniquity, which is self-will
(see also Ezekiel 28:12-19; Isaiah 14:9-20).

The author of fear, satan, is constantly
attempting to get you to yield to fear, or
bring intense pressure of extreme fear upon
you through terror. Terrorism is the purposeful use of fear as a weapon. Those
who use terror in that manner didn't learn
it from God, but from the spirit that gave
birth to fear, which is satan.

The following is an interesting story told
by Eliphaz the Temanite to Job:

Now a word was secretly brought to me, and my ear received a whisper of it. **In disquieting thoughts** *from the visions of the night,* **when deep sleep falls on men, fear came upon me, and trembling, which made all my bones shake.** *Then a spirit passed before my face;* **the hair on my body stood up.** *It stood still, but* **I could not discern its appearance.** *A form was before my eyes; there was silence; then I heard a voice saying...* (Job 4:12-16).

If you keep reading the following few verses, this spirit never said, "Fear not!" which is the charge all angels sent from God always give. This was a demonic spirit, possibly even satan himself, as he had taken extreme interest in Job as revealed in the first two chapters of the Book of Job.

The words I highlighted in the passage from Job 4 indicate that this spirit wanted Eliphaz to be scared out of his wits and made no attempt to assuage his fear at all. This is not the way God works, nor is it the way we see God's angels working throughout the Bible.

Now let's quickly plug something in while this is fresh on our minds. We go to Hebrews 11:6 and notice what it says: *"But **without faith it is impossible to please Him**, for he who comes to God must believe that He is, and that He is a rewarder of those who diligently seek Him."*

Without faith it is impossible to please God! If faith is what it takes to please God and receive from Him, then why would He ever want us to be in fear or afraid when He wants to speak to us or minister to us?

Notice what it says about all of God's angels in Hebrews 1:13-14:

> *"But to which of the angels has He ever said: 'Sit at My right hand, till I make Your enemies Your footstool'?* ***Are they not all ministering spirits sent forth to minister*** *for those who will inherit salvation?"*

Angels are *"ministering spirits sent forth to minister"* and they are not going to be able to do that if you and I are afraid and fearful in their presence. They will always tell us not to be afraid! Our enemy will never do that because he wants us to be afraid in his presence. Fear is to him what faith is to God. It pleases the devil when we are afraid.

Let's look at another clue about fear in 1 John 4:16-18:

And we have known and believed the love that God has for us. God is love, and he who abides in love abides in God, and God in him. **Love has been perfected among us in this: that we may have boldness in the day of judgment; because as He is, so are we in this world. There is no fear in love; but perfect love casts out fear, because fear involves torment. But he who fears has not been made perfect in love.**

This passage shows that God's love for us is a key to getting rid of fear. I will bring this up later in this study. However, notice that our ability to be bold and not fearful in the day of judgment is due to our union with Jesus Christ and through that union we are exactly like Him. First Corinthians

6:17 says, *"But he who is joined to the Lord is one spirit with Him."*

A major point to notice in the passage from 1 John 4 is found in the phrase: *"fear involves torment."* Many places in the Gospel accounts of Jesus' ministry describe people who were tormented by demonic spirits and various diseases. Acts 10:38 is very clear on this point: *"how God anointed Jesus of Nazareth with the Holy Spirit and with power, who went about doing good and **healing all who were oppressed by the devil**, for God was with Him."*

Demon spirits, sickness and disease, and other afflictions are satanic oppression and are described repeatedly as torments. Oppression and depression are the results of fear and designed to bring torment. And satan is behind all of it! Not God!

God brings judgment upon all who lived in obedience to satan's rule and influence. We read something very interesting in Revelation 21:8:

> *But the **cowardly**, unbelieving, abominable, murderers, sexually immoral, sorcerers, idolaters, and all liars shall have their part in the lake which burns with fire and brimstone, which is the second death.*

In the King James Version and other translations as well, the word "cowardly" is rendered "fearful." God judged fear through what Jesus did in His redemptive work. Those who are consumed with fear have not come to know the delivering power of the love of God as accomplished through the sacrifice of His Son on the

Cross. Those who live lives of fear and are consumed with fear, have no faith at all.

That is why, for believers, it is imperative to remove fear from our lives and walk free from it. It is not of God, at all!

Session 1

Study Guide

1. Fear   and   terror   do   not   come from _____ —it comes from _____.

2. There is a godly fear that is based in _____ honor.

3. 1 John 4 shows us the key to getting rid of fear is the _____ of _____.

4. Fear has _____.

It is impossible to please God without faith. So, whenever we approach God in prayer we need to always do it in faith—not fear.

Prayer

Father, I thank You that You are not the source or creator of fear. You have given me Your faith, and I use that faith to approach You now. Thank You that because of Your righteousness, and my union with Jesus Christ that brought me into Your righteousness, I have been made free from fear! Fear may approach me, but it is not coming from You! I thank You for that Lord, in Jesus' name, amen!

Session 2

Different Types of Fear

We are all familiar with the obvious type of fear that has an extreme physical and emotional response; something that comes out of the blue, unexpected, and literally scares us. But there are other manifestations of fear that are far more subtle, and actually far more dangerous.

Terror is an extreme form of fear that is seen in many parts of the world. It is a form of fear that can be used as a weapon. That is what terrorism is, the deliberate use of fear as a weapon. This type of fear is imposed upon people, both directly and indirectly. In a direct way, terror is used on individuals or a group of individuals with the threat of torture or death for some stated or unstated reason or purpose. This is actually a means to an end.

The indirect use of terror is a form of psychological warfare intended to cause a larger body of people, usually a government or nation, to capitulate to the demands of the terrorist. It is a form of weapon designed to accomplish a political religious goal born of extreme prejudice or hatred.

There are twelve different Hebrew words that are translated as fear or terror; or related words connected to fear and terror. This study is not going to breakdown all the different forms of fear covered in those words, but it is interesting to note that they encompass the full spectrum of the power of fear to influence people, many times suddenly.

In the Greek language of the Bible there is only one word translated terror, and that word is *phobos*. It is interesting that you can readily recognize that this word is the word we directly connect to fear, in that we call fear a "phobia." The list of phobias is too long and extensive to get into in this study. Suffice to say that there is a fear of just about everything you can imagine!

What needs to be gleaned from any study of those fears is that we learn that the vast majority of people, born again or not, are far more motivated by fear than they are by faith. I believe that events even of recent times in this world shows that this is the sad truth.

As I was preparing for a teaching series on fear one day, the Lord spoke to me and told me that it is not the outward, obvious fears that do the most harm. He said as damaging as those kinds of fears can be, even those that come up suddenly, the most dangerous form of fear is subtle and operates without any noticeable emotion or feeling. I want to address this subtle fear with a closer look because the New Testament identifies this kind of fear as being spiritually dangerous.

Fear Through Worry

Many believers struggle with their faith walk due to not understanding, or not taking seriously, the danger of entertaining the spirit of fear through worry. This dimension of fear is subtle, many times operating subconsciously, and undermines your ability to have strong faith.

Worry, in so many different ways, can be the legal avenue that the adversary can land manifestations of the curse in your life and it be completely ignored due to not understanding the open door worry grants the one who wants to steal, kill, and destroy your life.

I want to point out the reality of what I am teaching you by looking at Proverbs 26:2: *"Like a flitting sparrow, like a flying swallow, so a curse without cause shall not alight."*

The King James Version of the Bible renders the last part of this verse this way, *"so the curse causeless shall not come."* Other translations use a variety of descriptive language here, but they all imply that a curse will not land unless something legal granted it that right. What would be legal in the light of what we are discussing in this study? Any form of fear, but especially that which is subtle and continually engaged in, such as worry.

Let's look at this from a very familiar passage of Scripture, Job 1:1-5:

> *There was a man in the land of Uz, whose name was Job; and that man was blameless and upright, and one who feared God and shunned evil. And seven sons and three daughters were born to him. Also, his possessions were seven thousand sheep, three thousand camels, five hundred yoke of oxen, five hundred female donkeys, and a very large household, so that this man was the greatest of all the people of the East.*
>
> *And his sons would go and feast in their houses, each on his appointed day, and would send and invite their three sisters to eat and drink with them. **So it was, when the days of feasting had run their course, that Job would send and sanctify them, and he would rise early***

in the morning and offer burnt offerings according to the number of them all. For Job said, "It may be that my sons have sinned and cursed God in their hearts." Thus Job did regularly."

I highlighted verse 5 for this reveals that Job was not sacrificing in faith, but out of fear. Notice he said, *"It may be…."* He didn't know for sure. And, *"Thus Job did regularly."* The Hebrew language here indicates he was doing this over and over, continually. This is what worry looks like.

When you read verses 6-12 in Job 1, you find the scene shifts to Heaven and satan lands an accusation against Job. He did this because he knew that in spite of God's hedge protecting Job and all that he had, the devil brought up that he had a legal right to move in on Job. Verses 11 and 12 reveal the charge he leveled against Job:

"But now, stretch out Your hand and touch all that he has, and he will surely curse You to Your face!" And the Lord said to Satan, "Behold, all that he has is in your power; only do not lay a hand on his person." So Satan went out from the presence of the Lord.

God did not remove the hedge to let the devil work out on Job. Job removed the hedge and satan knew it. Ecclesiastes 10:8 says, *"He who digs a pit will fall into it, and whoever breaks through a wall will be bitten by a serpent."* The King James Version renders that last part this way, *"whoso breaketh an hedge, a serpent shall bite him."*

That is exactly what happened to Job. His constant worry and fear over his children possibly sinning and cursing God tore the hedge that God had put up around him to protect Job—and the serpent himself, satan, took full advantage of the opening.

We read the story play out with four breaking news events hitting Job's ears as one messenger after another describe one disaster and calamity after another befalling Job's family and property. The curse, without a legal right to land, shall not come.

Jumping over a lot of material in Job chapters 1 and 2 to compress our study to the main theme, I want to point out that based upon Job 1:21, Job apparently had no knowledge of an enemy and adversary in the realm of the spirit that had brought all the destruction: *"Naked I came from my mother's womb, and naked shall I return there. The Lord gave, and the Lord has taken away; blessed be the name of the Lord."*

We can read that it was not God who took away anything from Job, God had given Job everything he lost to the thief who is the devil. God did not give the devil permission, either. God could not pervert justice when there had clearly been fear and anxiety in Job over his family. That is what allowed the attack—fear.

Notice what Job says in chapter 3:25-26: *"For the thing I greatly feared has come upon me, and what I dreaded has happened to me. I am not at ease, nor am I quiet; I have no rest, for trouble comes."*

That is the way fear works! It attracts the very thing you are worried about. The word "dread" as is defined as "great fear, or apprehension of evil or danger. It expresses more than fear, and less than terror or fright. It is an uneasiness or alarm excited by expected pain, loss or other evil."[1]

Job was not believing God to protect his family or himself at this point. He was in fear. And that was the legal avenue that allowed the devil to move in and steal, kill, and to destroy.

Fear Tolerated Is Faith Contaminated

Jesus taught about the absolute necessity to stop fear, worry, and anxiety in our lives. He knew, as we are having to learn, that *fear tolerated is faith contaminated*. In other words, your faith will not work when you are yielding to fear of any kind.

So as we develop this concept of the subtle and hidden fear that can trip us up, let's see what Jesus had to say about this kind of fear. Mark 4:14-19.

> *"The sower sows the word. And these are the ones by the wayside where the*

*word is sown. When they hear, Satan comes immediately and takes away the word that was sown in their hearts. These likewise are the ones sown on stony ground who, when they hear the word, immediately receive it with gladness; and they have no root in themselves, and so endure only for a time. Afterward, when tribulation or persecution arises for the word's sake, immediately they stumble. Now these are the ones sown among thorns; they are the ones who hear the word, and **the cares of this world**, the deceitfulness of riches, and the desires for other things **entering in choke the word, and it becomes unfruitful**"* (Mark 4:14-19).

This is so important. Jesus reveals in verse 15 that the devil comes to steal the Word of God out of our heart immediately after we hear it. Why? Because the Word carries the power. God's Word is the conducting medium of God's power! If satan can steal the Word out of our heart before it can take root and start producing its power and life in our lives, he removes us as a threat to his operation.

If we successfully keep cultivating the Word in our lives to the point that it starts producing results, the enemy will go to a more subtle and less obvious strategy than persecution and affliction to try and steal the word. This is what Jesus reveals in verses 18-19: *"Now these are the ones sown among thorns; they are the ones who hear the word, and **the cares of this world**, the deceitfulness of riches, and the desires for other things entering in choke the word, and it becomes unfruitful."*

Notice the phrase *"the cares of this world"* and understand what this is revealing to us.

The key word here is *"care."* Many translations render this as "anxious care" indicating that this is a fear-based concern. The Greek word for care is *merimna* and it carries a meaning of being distracted; being worried, or under mental pressure.

Let's look at Mark 4:18 in the light of the meaning of this word *"care"*:

> *"Now these are the ones sown among thorns; they are the ones who hear the word, and the [anxious, fear-based, worry and concern to the point of being distracted] cares of this world, the deceitfulness of riches, and the desires for other things entering in choke the word, and it becomes unfruitful."*

This kind of care is not being responsible in a good way; it is a distraction and meditation in fear-based thoughts. *Worry is meditation energized by fear.* You can have no peace with this kind of thought life. And, worry and anxiety are designed by the enemy to cause the Word of God to become unfruitful, or ineffective, in your life. That is not what you want to happen!

When you look through the New Testament, you that see we are given explicit instructions on how to deal with "care" and its related forms. Take note of Philippians 4:6-7:

> **Be anxious for nothing**, but in every-thing by prayer and supplication, with thanksgiving, let your requests be made known to God; and the peace of God, which surpasses all understanding, will guard your hearts and minds through Christ Jesus.

The New Living Translation renders the phrase *"Be anxious for nothing"* as *"Don't worry about anything."*

Now let's look at something Jesus says in Matthew 6:25-34 quoted here from the Amplified Bible, Classic Edition:

> *Therefore I tell you, **stop being perpetually uneasy (anxious and worried) about your life**, what you shall eat or what you shall drink; or about your body, what you shall put on. Is not life greater [in quality] than food, and the body [far above and more excellent] than clothing? Look at the birds of the air; they neither sow nor reap nor gather into barns, and yet your heavenly Father keeps feeding them. Are you not worth much more than they?*

*And **who of you by worrying and being anxious** can add one unit of measure* (cubit) *to his stature or to the span of his life? And **why should you be anxious** about clothes? Consider the lilies of the field and learn thoroughly how they grow; they neither toil nor spin. Yet I tell you, even Solomon in all his magnificence* (excellence, dignity, and grace) *was not arrayed like one of these. But if God so clothes the grass of the field, which today is alive and green and tomorrow is tossed into the furnace, will He not much more surely clothe you, O you of little faith?*

***Therefore do not worry and be anxious, saying,** What are we going to have to eat? or, What are we going to have to drink? or, What are we going to have to wear? For the Gentiles* (heathen) *wish for and crave and* *diligently seek all these things, and your heavenly Father knows well that you need them all.*

But seek (aim at and strive after) *first of all His kingdom and His righteousness* (His way of doing and being right), *and then all these things taken together will be given you besides.* **So do not worry or be anxious about tomorrow,** *for tomorrow will have worries and anxieties of its own. Sufficient for each day is its own trouble.*

This entire passage is actually instructions to born-again believers on what not to do if you are living in the Kingdom of God. Stop all the worrying! Get rid of the anxiety and fear! And don't let the fear, worry, and anxiety get into your mind or proceed from your mouth!

*For God has **not** given us a spirit of fear, but of **power** and of **love** and of a **sound mind*** (2 Timothy 1:7).

You have been delivered out of the kingdom of darkness (see Colossians 1:12-13), you have not been given a spirit of fear (see Romans 8:14-16), and Jesus has already paid the price for you to walk free from the fear of death and from the power of the devil (see Hebrews 2:14-15).

You have a legal right to live fear-free! This benefit of the Kingdom of God is not automatic, but it is available. It is up to you to choose what you are going think about, speak, and act upon. The Holy Spirit will lead you, but you must learn to yield to His leadership. He will not overpower your choices.

Note

1. Webster's Dictionary 1828, s.v. "dread," http://webstersdictionary1828.com/ Dictionary/dread; accessed March 30, 2020.

Session 2

Study Guide

1. Terror is the deliberate use of fear as a _____.

2. The Greek word for fear is _____.

3. According to Proverbs 26:2, the curse without a _____ cannot land.

4. Worry is a form of _____.

5. The _____ of the world will choke the _____ and cause the _____ to become _____.

6. We are not to _____ or be _____ about anything.

Prayer

Father, in the name of Jesus I declare today that I refuse to fear! I will not be anxious or worry about anything. I will trust and have faith in You for all of my needs! I determine that when I recognize I am worrying about or carrying the care of anything, I will cast that care over on You, and trust You to work it out in my favor! Amen!

Session 3

Step One to Freedom:
Securing a New Identity

The "new birth" is step one to your freedom from fear. When you accept Jesus as your Lord, God intends you to enjoy tremendous benefits and advantages that were lost by Adam when he sinned in the Garden of Eden. The changing of your spirit from death to life is the first step of victory over all the ills that have afflicted humankind since the day of Adam's fall.

One of the first identifiable spirit forces that afflicted humankind upon Adam's sin is fear. I refer you to Genesis 3:8-10 (NASB):

They heard the sound of the Lord God walking in the garden in the cool of the day, and the man and his wife hid themselves from the presence of the Lord God among the trees of the garden. Then the Lord God called to the man, and said to him, "Where are you?" He said, "I heard the sound of You in the garden, and I was afraid because I was naked; so I hid myself."

Adam and Eve hid because they were afraid. This word "afraid" in the Hebrew is the root word yare and has only one meaning—"to fear, to be afraid."[1] As applied in this context the word is referring to having fear and apprehension, which means "fear; suspicion; the prospect of future evil, accompanied with uneasiness of mind."[2]

When Adam stepped over into the realm of spiritual death, his faith took a reciprocal turn and began to function in reverse; this opposite, but certainly not equal force, is what we know as fear. We already referred to 2 Timothy 1:7, but let's look at it again from the Amplified Version, Classic Edition:

> *For God did not give us a spirit of timidity* (of cowardice, of craven and cringing and fawning fear), *but [He has given us a spirit] of power and of love and of calm and well-balanced mind and discipline and self-control.*

The spirit of fear and timidity did not come from God, it came from satan, as already mentioned in Session 1.

Second Corinthians 5:17-21 is a key passage to spend some time meditating and confessing to build it into your mind. Let's read it and then unpack some important points:

Therefore, **if anyone is in Christ, he is a new creation; old things have passed away; behold, all things have become new. Now all things are of God,** *who has reconciled us to Himself through Jesus Christ, and has given us the ministry of reconciliation, that is, that God was in Christ reconciling the world to Himself, not imputing their trespasses to them, and has committed to us the word of reconciliation. Now then, we are ambassadors for Christ, as though God were pleading through us: we implore you on Christ's behalf, be reconciled to God.* **For He made Him who knew no sin to be sin for us, that we might become the righteousness of God in Him.**

When you were born again—or in other words, were saved—you asked Jesus to come into your heart; you prayed a prayer for Jesus to take over your life; and you became a new creation, a new species of being that is now in union with Jesus Christ Himself by the indwelling presence of the Holy Spirit. (See 1 Corinthians 6:17; John 14:16-17.) You are now "in Christ" and He is now in you.

Being born again is critical to be able to see the bondage of fear broken away from your life! Notice that 2 Corinthians 5:17-18 declare old things are passed away, all things have become new, and all things now are of God—this refers to you as a spirit being. Spiritually you are completely new! The old sinner you used to be has been recreated and now you have been made the righteousness of God through union with Christ! You have a new identity and this new creation being you have become is not a creature of fear—you are a spiritual being able to live a life of faith and victory!

There are several other passages I want to point you to for you to understand the change that took place in your spirit the moment you received Jesus as your Lord. Ephesians 2:1-3 says:

> And you **He made alive**, who were dead in trespasses and sins, in which you once walked according to the course of this world, according to the prince of the power of the air, the spirit who now works in the sons of disobedience, among whom also we all once conducted ourselves in the lusts of our flesh, fulfilling the desires of the flesh and of the mind, and were by nature children of wrath, just as the others (See also Ephesians 2:11-13.)

As the first three verses from Ephesians 2 reveal, you were spiritually dead, but now you are alive in Christ. While you were spiritually dead—in a state of not drawing on God as the Source of your life—you were living your life according to the influences and passions that govern life in the world, independent of a spiritual union with Jesus Christ. Your very nature was one of sin, living with a subconscious fear of judgment and condemnation. That fear was what, even now, rules the world without a spiritual union with God through Jesus. (See Hebrews 2:14-15.)

Faith, Not Fear

Now, though, you are born of God, designed to live by the faith that was gifted to you through the new birth, and living in fear should be a thing of the past! (See

1 John 5:1-5; Ephesians 2:8-10; Galatians 2:20.)

You have also been born again by the incorruptible seed of the Word of God. (See 1 Peter 1:23.) Based on what we learn about the Word of God and faith from Romans 10:17, *So then faith comes by hearing, and hearing by the word of God,* God's Word is the source of faith! God's Word is the conductive medium of God's power, which is released and activated by faith. You are now a spirit designed by God to live by faith! You aren't just to use faith; you are to live every moment of every day being energized and empowered by the force and spirit of faith!

So, some questions are probably coming to you in the light of what you are learning up to this point, perhaps along this line of thinking:

- "Why, if this is true, do I still deal with so much fear?"

- "Where is the fear I experience coming from?"

- "How can I experience true freedom from fear and live a life of faith and victory?"

Those are good questions, and I will be giving you some pointers along the way through the rest of this study to discover the answers.

Let's take a look at 1 Thessalonians 5:23, *"Now may the God of peace Himself sanctify you completely; and may your **whole spirit, soul, and body** be preserved blameless at the coming of our Lord Jesus Christ."* Notice this breakdown by the Holy Spirit through the apostle Paul that describes your makeup as a human being created by God. You are a *spirit*; you have a *soul*, made up of your mind, emotions, and your will; and you live in a physical *body*.

It was your spirit that was born again, not your soul or your body. Your soul—mind, emotions, and will—has to be renewed through confession and meditation on the Word of God, the Bible. You have to renew your mind. God can only assist you in that process when you engage in it with discipline, diligence, and determination. We will discuss this in our next session.

Your physical body did not change, it was not reborn on the day you became a new creation. In fact, let's look at Romans 8:19-23 for a moment and discover a very important New Testament truth:

*For the earnest expectation of the creation eagerly waits for the revealing of the sons of God. For the creation was subjected to futility, not willingly, but because of Him who subjected it in hope; because the creation itself also will be delivered from the bondage of corruption into the glorious liberty of the children of God. For we know that the whole creation groans and labors with birth pangs together until now. Not only that, but **we also who have the first fruits of the Spirit, even we ourselves groan within ourselves, eagerly waiting for the adoption, the redemption of our body.***

What pertains to this physical realm, including your physical body, has yet to experience deliverance, which was secured through the redemptive work of the Cross by Jesus Christ. According to the New Testament, your physical body is corrupt, dishonorable, weak, natural, and earthy. (See 1 Corinthians 15:42-47.) In fact, 1 Corinthians 15:50 plainly states this fact, *"Now this I say, brethren, that flesh and blood cannot inherit the kingdom of God; nor does corruption inherit incorruption."*

The weakest part of your triune makeup is your physical body. First John 2:15-17 gives you some understanding with regard to this truth:

> *Do not love the world or the things in the world. If anyone loves the world, the love of the Father is not in him. For all that is in the world—**the lust of the flesh, the lust of the eyes, and the pride of life**—is not of the Father but is of the world. And the world is passing*

away, and the lust of it; but he who does the will of God abides forever.

To define "lust" in a non-religious way, we can describe it as pressure; in fact, it is the pressure of temptation. Notice the three avenues of temptation as listed in this Scripture passage: 1) the pressure that comes through the flesh; 2) the pressure that comes through what you see with the eyes; and 3) the pressure that comes upon the mind that leads to self-willed actions independent of the leading of the Holy Spirit. As the last part of this passage states, only those who do the will of God will experience true victory. That means you are being led by the Holy Spirit and not yielding to temptation or stepping out in self-willed pride.

Fear uses all three of these points of temptation to, at the very least, to lure you into thinking and meditating on the thoughts and images the enemy wants you to act on. Fear is most of the time subtle, and occasionally completely overt and intense. To be permanently free from fear, you have to break the strongholds in your mind and revoke the legal rights the enemy has to continually keep the pressure of temptation on you to yield to fear.

Mind renewal will deal with the strongholds, but first you must learn to recognize the things that are at the root of life-long battles with fear. This is an area that will not yield to what is known as spiritual warfare. If it is legal in nature, you will have to step by faith into the Court of Heaven and legally remove the iniquity that has been generational in your bloodline where fear is concerned. Iniquity is the legal right in the bloodline the enemy uses to keep pushing any sin or transgression down a family tree.

Iniquity is the generational sin that allows the adversary the right to deny you your destiny and rob you of your God-given inheritance and purpose. Iniquity started generations ago, and has had time to develop a mindset that is passed down in the family and literally shapes the identity of entire families. Where fear is concerned, the iniquity of fear in the bloodline can lead to fear being the tool and means of training of each successive generation as they are born and grow up. This kind of influence of fear is dangerous because it is hidden, subtle, and operates below the level of conscious awareness.

If you were raised in a household where fear was a tool of training, rather than being trained and instructed from a spirit of love and faith, you probably struggle with fear, worry, anxiety, depression, and other mental and emotional issues that essentially self-sabotage your ability to move into the fullness of God's purpose and destiny for your life. That kind of culture of fear, in all likelihood, is rooted in iniquity in the generational bloodline of your family, and is not your fault. You have a right to be free from it.

You do this by very simply repenting on behalf of your generational past for allowing fear to be the ruling spiritual power in your family. Ask for the blood of Jesus to speak and remit and remove that iniquity out of you and your bloodline. And ask that the legal right granted to the enemy to torment you and your family because of that iniquity to be revoked. Ask for that precious Blood to silence the voice of fear in your life and family, forever.

One final word on your identity in Christ. This is actually an entire study in and of itself. You will discover that there are well over 130 verses in the New Testament, primarily the New Testament letters, that use the phrases *"in Christ," "through Christ," "in Him," "in whom," "through whom,"* etc. Those phrases are not just talking about Jesus—each is referring to you too. First Corinthians 6:17 says, *"But he who is joined to the Lord is one spirit with Him."* You and the Lord became one with each other through a spiritual union that miraculously took place when you were born again. You are not a forgiven sinner, you are a new creation in Christ! You have been made the righteousness of God through that union—and your new identity is discovered in Him!

In Him there is no fear! In Him there is no anxiety, worry, depression, or any other emotional or mental oppression. Fear does not exist in Christ! So, it should not exist in you! He became one with all of us on the Cross and bore all of that for you on the Cross, so that you can receive and enjoy all that is in Him through union with Him.

The new birth experience is not just a ticket to avoid hell, it is the beginning of a life of victory, peace, and joy unspeakable! You may still have challenges and battles, but you have the means and ability, through Jesus Christ, to come out on top every time! That is why we must learn who we are in Christ and change our identity to who we have become in and through Him!

Notes

1. H.W.F. Gesenius, *Gesenius' Hebrew and Chaldee Lexicon to the Old Testament Scriptures* (Grand Rapids, MI: Baker Book House, 1990), s.v. #3372, (1), 364.

2. Webster's Dictionary 1828, "afraid"; http://webstersdictionary1828.com/Dictionary/afraid; accessed April 1, 2020.

Session 3

Study Guide

1. The _____ is step one to my freedom from fear.

2. When Adam sinned in the Garden of Eden he became _____.

3. In Christ I have become a new _____.

4. I have been made the _____ of _____ through union with Christ.

5. I am a _____; I have a _____; and I live in a physical _____.

6. In Christ there is no _____!

Prayer

Lord Jesus, I am in You, and You are in me. We are one spirit with each other. You are my Lord and my Righteous Judge, and I come before You right now and ask that You would accept my repentance for any and all generational fear in me and my bloodline. I ask that the Blood that speaks for me in Heaven's Court would remove and remit that iniquity; and revoke any legal right the adversary had to accuse me, or bring a case against me in an attempt to deny me my freedom and deliverance. Thank You for this, Lord Jesus! I declare that I am free from the generational iniquity of fear! Amen!

Session 4

Step Two to Freedom: Learning to Renew the Mind

Did you know that after you get born again the first assignment that you have is to renew your mind? Did you know that this is a life-long endeavor that you actually will never fully accomplish? Have you ever been taught or instructed on how to renew your mind and what its purpose is? And, finally, do you know the signs or indications that you are making progress in the mind renewal process?

After forty years of ministry and over a quarter of a century of being a teacher and pastor, I can honestly say that the biggest key to a successful life in Christ is learning to renew the mind to the Word of God. Those who have taken up the discipline and dedication of renewing their minds are the ones I've seen personally develop and grow into powerful and productive citizens of the Kingdom of God. Those who don't renew their minds struggle with all kinds of issues and continually battle all kinds of issues that they never seem to be able to control or overcome.

I am going to give you in this session some of the major keys to mind renewal that you can apply immediately and begin to see the power of the Word of God and the power of the Holy Spirit. These keys will help create within you a brand-new way of thinking, developing on a foundational level the very mind of Christ! I will show you the scriptural basis for this shortly.

What Mind Renewal Is *Not*

I want to share with you up-front what mind renewal is *not*, for I don't want you to waste time doing something that does not necessarily produce real results.

Mind renewal is not Scripture memorization! I repeat—mind renewal is not memorizing Bible verses. You will certainly build into your memory the verses that you are using to renew your mind, but that is not the goal of mind renewal. I know people who have memorized vast volumes of the Bible who still think predominately in line with the world's way of living rather than God's Kingdom way of living in freedom.

Memorization is approaching life by installing facts as opposed to renewing your mind to actually have a change of culture mentally, where you are thinking more and more on an ever-increasing manner in line with the mind of Christ.

We all have inherited mindsets from our parents, families, localized culture of where we were raised from our childhood, and other surrounding influences that from our birth installed a mindset that we had very little or no control over the programming. This mindset consists of a complex, integrated way of thinking that consists of rules, values, beliefs, and standards that we largely did not choose of our own volition.

What Mind Renewal *Is*

When we are born again, we find that while we have experienced a very real encounter with a very real God, our lifestyle is governed by thinking, that for most believers is incompatible with the life of God. We become new creation people with an old sinner mindset. This is a problem. And if you don't immediately begin the process of renewing your mind, you will end up living a frustrated life wanting to live a life more reflective of what we see demonstrated in the life of Jesus or the believers in the Book of Acts.

As already pointed out in this course, your spirit was born again and is, even now, you are a new species of being—a new creation in Christ. But your mind did not get born again, and your body didn't change either. The writings of the apostle Paul reveal what we must do to begin to see the "transformation" from living as sinners to living a manner of life that becomes more and more expressive of the change that took place in our spirit.

Let's look at what Paul wrote and discuss some of these vital truths. We will start with this important passage from Ephesians 4:17-24 (New International Version):

> So I tell you this, and insist on it in the Lord, that **you must no longer live as the Gentiles do, in the futility of their thinking.** They are darkened in their understanding and separated from the life of God because of the ignorance that is in them due to the hardening of their hearts. Having lost all sensitivity, they have given themselves over to sensuality so as to indulge in every kind of impurity, and they are full of greed. **That, however, is not the way of life you learned when you heard about Christ and were taught in him in accordance with the truth that is in Jesus. You were taught, with regard to your former way of life, to put off your old self, which is being corrupted by its**

deceitful desires; to be made new in the attitude of your minds; and to put on the new self, created to be like God in true righteousness and holiness.

For however long you have lived in the world, learning its lifestyle and thinking based upon its standards, values, rules, and beliefs, that is how long you have been trained and disciplined in a manner of thinking, speaking, and living that is incompatible with the life of Christ. The mindset you possess on the day you are born again is the mindset that must change if you ever have any hope or desire to give expression to the true nature and Spirit of Jesus. This does not happen automatically, nor is it developed without discipline or effort on your part.

However, the Holy Spirit, who dwells within you, will engage with you in the process of mind renewal and accelerate the process with His help and influence. But you must engage with the Word of God and do your part.

You must *"put off your old self"* and put on the *"new self"* just like you would change out of a dirty set of clothes and put on a clean and new suit of clothes. This transformation is accomplished through the renewing of the mind. Notice this next passage from Colossians 3:5-11 (NASB):

> *Therefore consider the members of your earthly body as dead to immorality, impurity, passion, evil desire, and greed, which amounts to idolatry. For it is because of these things that the wrath of God will come upon the sons of disobedience, and **in them you also once walked, when you were living in***

them. But now you also, put them all aside: anger, wrath, malice, slander, and abusive speech from your mouth. Do not lie to one another, since you laid aside the old self with its evil practices, and have put on the new self who is being renewed to a true knowledge *according to the image of the One who created him—a renewal in which there is no distinction between Greek and Jew, circumcised and uncircumcised, barbarian, Scythian, slave and freeman, but Christ is all, and in all.*

Can you see the pattern? You are to put off the old self and corrupt way of thinking, and put on the new self, which is in union with Jesus. Mind renewal is what allows you to begin to live from the inside-out, no longer keeping rules and regulations of a religious nature that are only an outside-in kind of lifestyle. Remember, you have the Holy Spirit dwelling within you, and He wants you to be influenced and energized through and by His impulses, not the impulses of the world around you, or your fleshly passions.

Look at this next passage from Romans, one that is the key we must take seriously and engage in with our faith and agreement to see transformation take place:

> *Therefore I urge you, brethren, by the mercies of God, to present your bodies a living and holy sacrifice, acceptable to God, which is your spiritual service of worship. And **do not be conformed to this world, but be transformed by the renewing of your mind**, so that you may prove what the will of God is, that*

which is good and acceptable and perfect
(Romans 12:1-2 NASB).

The simple truth is that if you do not renew your mind to the way of thinking that agrees with the Kingdom of God culture—which is the Word of God, especially the New Testament—you will continue to live a life that is conformed to the world system and its corrupt way of thinking and behaving. There is another rendering of this verse that is particularly expressive of the importance of mind renewal found in The Message Bible:

> *So here's what I want you to do, God helping you: Take your everyday, ordinary life—your sleeping, eating, going-to-work, and walking-around life— and place it before God as an offering. Embracing what God does for you*

is the best thing you can do for him.
**Don't become so well-adjusted to
your culture that you fit into it without even thinking. Instead, fix your
attention on God. You'll be changed
from the inside out. Readily recognize what he wants from you, and
quickly respond to it. Unlike the
culture around you, always dragging
you down to its level of immaturity,
God brings the best out of you, devel-
ops well-formed maturity in you**
(Romans 12:1-2).

I want to emphasize that when we are
born again we enter into the Kingdom
of God with mindsets that are very well
adjusted to the culture of the world; the
mindsets that were installed into our subconscious thinking that are largely based on
a life lived independent of Jesus, the Holy

Spirit, and the culture of Heaven. We *must* change to a new way of thinking to be truly used of God and walk in all the fullness that Jesus paid such an awesome price to bring into this earth by way of the Cross!

Again, fear is incompatible with the heavenly Kingdom culture, which is totally a culture of faith that works by and through the power of agape love. We honor God, Jesus, and the Holy Spirit. That honor is not fear-based as in being afraid of God. We have a deep respect and reverential honor of Him, but at the same time He is approachable—our Father and Friend who loves us beyond any ability to describe or understand it.

How to Renew Your Mind

So how do we renew the mind? Quite simply it is done through meditation on the

Word of God, and then purposefully confessing the Word of God to "install" the Word deep into your inner self, especially the subconscious mind. This type of confession is not so much a "faith confession" as it is a deliberate and purposeful feeding of the Word into the mind and spirit to put within our true selves the conductive medium of God's power, which is the Word of God. That is how we provide the Holy Spirit the material He needs to be able to cause the transformation to take place in our thinking and in our behavior.

You may have never thought about this in the following manner, but you know and understand that your physical body, in order to grow, develop, and become strong and healthy, needs a regular and proper diet. The same is true of your soul and spirit— the real you. (See 1 Thessalonians 5:23.)

Your spirit needs food in order to grow, develop, and become strong in faith and love. The Holy Spirit needs your cooperation to enable your spiritual development to take place under His supervision. First Peter 2:2 says, *"as newborn babes, desire the pure milk of the word, that you may grow thereby...."* Spiritual growth is supported and energized through a steady, regular diet of the Word of God. Not just reading it, but feeding on it through confession and meditation.

The following are three Scripture passages that express the importance of meditation:

Joshua 1:8 (AMPC): **"This Book of the Law shall not depart out of your mouth, but you shall meditate on it day and night,** *that you may observe* *and do according to all that is written in it. For then you shall make your way prosperous, and then you shall deal wisely and have good success."*

Psalm 1:1-3 (AMPC): *"Blessed (happy, fortunate, prosperous, and enviable) is the man who walks and lives not in the counsel of the ungodly [following their advice, their plans and purposes], nor stands [submissive and inactive] in the path where sinners walk, nor sits down [to relax and rest] where the scornful [and the mockers] gather. But his delight and desire are in the law of the Lord, and **on His law (the precepts, the instructions, the teachings of God) he habitually meditates (ponders and studies) by day and by night.** And he shall be like a tree firmly planted [and tended] by the streams of water, ready to bring forth its* *fruit in its season; its leaf also shall not fade or wither; and everything he does shall prosper [and come to maturity].*"

1 Timothy 4:14-16: "*Do not neglect the gift that is in you, which was given to you by prophecy with the laying on of the hands of the eldership.* **Meditate on these things; give yourself entirely to them, that your progress may be evident to all.** *Take heed to yourself and to the doctrine. Continue in them, for in doing this you will save both yourself and those who hear you.*"

Meditation involves confession—out loud so you can hear it—muttering the Word to yourself, thinking deeply and intently on the Word, and through and by your imagination, picturing in your mind what the Word is communicating to you. See yourself doing it, possessing it, or living it, on purpose and regularly. Meditating should be done daily for it to begin to bring a change in your thinking and take root.

An additional help to this is to pray in the Spirit while thinking about the Word. This engages the Holy Spirit in the process and releases even greater revelation and the latent power of the Word to influence the change in your subconscious mind, where the change must take place.

This is challenging work, but the rewards are literally unmeasurable and builds over time to establish divine strongholds in your mind that are virtually impossible for the enemy to overcome. If you do what is taught in this session and commit to feeding your spirit God's Word, fear will lose its grip over your life from the inside-out.

Session 4

Study Guide

1. Mind renewal is not _____.

2. My spirit was born again, but my _____ and my _____ did not.

3. Mind renewal is the way I put off the _____ and put on the _____.

4. _____ and _____ are the two main components of mind renewal.

5. My spirit gets _____ as I renew my _____.

6. I get the best results when I meditate on the _____ every day.

Prayer

Father, I commit today to confess and meditate on Your Word every day. I look forward to the benefits that confession and meditation of Your Word will bring into my life. Your Word is food for my spirit, and I am hungry, Lord! Thank You for Your Word! In Jesus' name, amen.

Session 5

Step Three to Freedom: Act on the Word, Even When Facing Fear

James 1:21-26 says:

> *Therefore lay aside all filthiness and overflow of wickedness, and **receive with meekness the implanted word, which is able to save your souls.** But be doers of the word, and not hearers only, deceiving yourselves. For if anyone is a hearer of the word and not a doer, he is like a man observing his natural face in a mirror; for he observes himself, goes*

*away, and immediately forgets what kind of man he was. But **he who looks into the perfect law of liberty and continues in it, and is not a forgetful hearer but a doer of the work, this one will be blessed in what he does. If anyone among you thinks he is religious, and does not bridle his tongue but deceives his own heart, this one's religion is useless.***

This session may be the shortest of the series of lessons, but it actually is the most important one of all. If you do not do what I have taught you in this series of lessons, you will not have freedom from fear. Apply the biblical wisdom to your life and stick with it—it will produce amazing results.

Notice the first part of this passage from James: *"receive with meekness the implanted word, which is able to save your souls."* When you start confessing and meditating on the Word of God, you are actually implanting it in your heart and bringing its saving power into your mind, emotions, and allowing it to influence your will. Your spirit is already "saved" through the new birth, but your soul has to have the implanted Word for what is in your spirit to begin to have the influence to direct your choices and produce right behavior. This is what mind renewal is all about!

The second part indicates two important steps. By being a *doer of the work* of mind renewal and identifying the generational iniquities that the enemy is using to introduce delays in your progress and getting rid of them through repentance, you will see progress like never before! You will not forget the Word you act on and get results with—because you didn't memorize it, you experienced it! That is the blessing of doing!

Also, this process begins to put a governor on your tongue. Your words rule you, and set the boundaries of your life. When you fill up with the Word, and see the change in your thinking, the Word of God will also influence your speech to be more of a language of faith, instead of fear. You will become aware of your words and recognize when you are speaking out of line with the language of faith. This is a huge benefit of this process!

Meditate on the *"in Christ"* verses. Meditate on the Scriptures that talk about God's love for you. Read 1 John 4:7-19 every day and meditate on it until it takes root inside you. *Psalm 91* needs to be installed in your subconscious mind deeply and strongly. *Psalm 23* is another important chapter of meditation and feeding. All of this together will flush the fear out of your subconscious mind and install a mind governed by faith and deep trust in the Lord who loves you, unconditionally. You will see change if you do this, I promise. ***Just do it!***

Session 5

Study Guide

1. If I will _____ the Word, and
   _____ with it, I will
   _____ amazing results.

2. Mind renewal is actually being a
   _____ of the Word.

3. I need to just _____!

Prayer

*Father, I commit to apply what I have
read and learned in this study. My life
of freedom from fear begins right now! I
am a doer of the Word and I, as a result,
will be blessed in my doing! I choose to*

speak words that agree with You and Your will for my life, and refuse to speak words of fear and worry, in Jesus' name! Amen!

About the Author

Dr. Bill Dennington is a seasoned minister who has been in active ministry since 1978; has pioneered two churches; and has traveled nationally and internationally speaking in churches, Bible schools, and at conferences. Bill and Lorie have been married since 1982 and have two children and three grandchildren. His daily devotionals, *Words for the Heart*, are viewed around the world on YouTube.

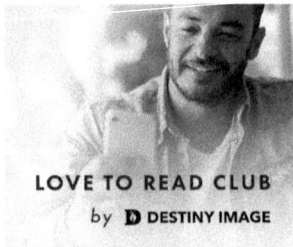

www.ingramcontent.com/pod-product-compliance
Lightning Source LLC
Chambersburg PA
CBHW070534030426
42337CB00016B/2195